MMA Cardio:

6 Week 16:8 Fasting Diet and Training,
UFC Cardio Conditioning, MMA Fitness, How To Build The MMA Body,
Building a MMA Physique, The MMA Workout

By

M Laurence

Table of Contents

Introduction

I want to thank you and congratulate you for purchasing the book "MAA Cardio".

This book contains a hardcore mix of Weight Training, Cardio and Yoga along with proven routines and strategies on how to become a lean, mean, fitness machine.

MMA is one of the biggest sports in the world to rival boxing, football and professional wrestling. Many people watch the MMA and various fight tournaments on TV because not only is it great entertainment but the physiques on show look great. They have an incredible mix of power and speed, strength and stamina.

It's also the aesthetics - the powerful legs, and lean arms, ripped chest, all tapering to and perhaps the most important - a taut 6-pack stomach.

Unlike some sort of steroid-jacked bodybuilder, the Mixed Martial Arts body is they are attainable. You can achieve this look if you put the work in.

My previous book 'How To Build The MAA Body' focused more on packing on size. But building muscle is only one part of the story. One half of the conversation of men's physique. It's also the often neglected part, and once mastered it can change your look dramatically in a big way. This book is designed to do just that.

Cardio is more than just a couple of jogs a week, it requires specific and general muscular strength, varying cardio workouts and rest and recuperation.

This book combines a varied and challenging 6 week training regime, with a healthy diet plan – with cheat days and the secret weapon to getting ripped: Intermittent Fasting. These three elements combine to create turbo-charged regime geared to burning fat and toning muscle. However if feel like you are not toning up and losing fat fast enough, don't get discouraged.

This is not an overnight solution, and it will take time. Your body will take time to adapt to the new fitness routines. This is completely normal. The intermittent fasting diet might be difficult at first and initially your body will wonder what's going on. If you are really struggling then feel free to stop and just concentrate on the diet and training. Then when you're ready phase in the fasting. I've added Yoga as the perfect bookend to hard training. This will stretch, relax and tone muscles. Recuperation is key to building muscle.

Here are my other books on MAA:

How To Build The MMA Body:
Paperback
https://www.createspace.com/6461161

KDP Version
https://www.amazon.com/dp/B01JBMB2N6

So let's get started. It's time for you to get to work!

1. Building The MMA Body

Let's start with Intermittent Fasting which has been banded around as some kind of savior to mankind. Is it really of any benefit?

Simple answer – yes. It is one of the best ways to get into shape by making the body burn fat while not eating. Now combine that with a high energy workout and weights regime and we can start to really sculpt a lean body.

I'm going to focus on the 16/8 Intermittent Fasting method.

How it works

You eat within a window of 8 hours, effectively squashing your 3 meals closer together and fast for 16 hours. The fast is where the magic happens. Once you push the body into a fasted state we begin to reap the benefits of Intermittent Fasting:

- Insulin levels: Blood levels of insulin drop significantly, which aids fat burning.
- Human growth hormone: The blood levels of growth hormone may increase as much as 5-fold. Higher levels of this hormone facilitate fat burning and muscle gain, and have many other benefits.
- Cellular repair: The body induces important cellular repair processes, such as removing waste material from cells.
- Gene expression: There are beneficial changes in several genes and molecules related to longevity and protection against disease.

The practice of fasting has been around as early as the 1940s and it hasn't been until recently that research has backed up that the true benefits of fasting.

Fasting + Exercise

We are enhancing and augmenting the fat burning capacity of fasting by incorporating exercise.

We want a visually pleasing MMA physique - strong legs, svelte arms, toned chest, lean back all tapering to and perhaps the most important - a tight taut flat stomach.

2. The Strategy

Let's go into detail about what we'll be doing.

3 Weeks - Weights, Cardio and Flexibility Cycle

Week 1

We utilize a three-week workout and repeat. Week 1 you will train the whole body once with weights and rest Sunday. We will also incorporate lots of walking - every day in fact. Plus running and some cardio routines. I want you to do light cardio in the morning because we're aiding the 'fasted state' our body is in, making it burn more fat.

Week 2

The second week is all about cardio and training body endurance. Again I urge you to walk every morning, sometimes we're going to run. Aim to increase walking where possible, it's one of the easiest exercises and safest exercises to do and it all counts. Again Sunday is a rest day and a cheat day, so you can relax and enjoy a cheat meal of your choice.

Week 3

For the third week, we'll be focusing on stretching and flexibility. Never stretch further than where your body aches, as this is about relaxing and working out any tightness in your body. This is also where we calm the mind before the storm. Each day try to extend yourself further and holding your stances longer. Since as we won't be building muscles, we won't be taking as much protein in our diet.

3 Weeks Cycle revisited

Weeks 4 – 6

One of the important things about a workout schedule is to be consistent. Consistency is king. Consistency will be with difference between you and the next guy. So for the latter 3 weeks, we'll go over the same schedule. Week 4 will be Weights, week 5 will be Cardio, and week 6 will be Yoga. The important difference is that these sessions will require you to do more than the original week. On the other hand, if you keep doing the same exercises for a long period of time, your body will 'adapt' and, while there may be big initial gains (muscle) and losses (fat), these will then come much more slowly with the same workout. So changes are built in.

Supersets to Size

If you're unfamiliar with Supersets- they are two exercises working opposite muscles. They are time-efficient method of training that we'll be using and also more intense. By doing sets back-to-back, you reduce your total workout time while still doing the same amount of total work.

Super setting is fantastic for pummeling antagonistic muscles - Back/Biceps, Chest/Triceps, Back/Chest and Biceps/Triceps and legs Hams/Glutes. Supersets increase Lactic Acid production, which helps boost Growth Hormone (GH) levels in the body. The body responds to the reduced pH (increased acidity) in the body from the production of Lactic Acid by secreting GH. GH is a powerful fat loss hormone.

Power and Intensity

We will be building muscle endurance which will therefore build strength and conditioning. This is done using tempo. By this I mean a 1 second pull/push/ on a given move - POWERFUL and with FORCE - and then under perfect control a 4 second release. The muscles are still working all the way. So we are changing the tempo, the speed of either the concentric (shortening) or eccentric (lengthening) component of the lift. There is no 'resting' at the bottom of any move. As soon as you are as close to the bottom of the move - you POWER back up for the 1 second concentric and again release for 4 second eccentric under your complete control.

You must have heard of the term TUT - Time Under Tension - there are a number of variations on the term, they all mean the same. It is the time your actual muscle is lifting or lowering under stress. You may find that you're actually only working your muscles for 5 minutes in an hour workout! With the 1 second concentric and 4 second eccentric move with no rest we work the muscle much harder for longer.

Many people will struggle with this at first as it's so common to do one arm curl, take a break/release all tension and do another. Even a split second rest is still a release of tension. Not good enough. You need to be working your muscles 100% of the time during a set. THEN you rest between sets.

So let's get to it!

3. Intermittent Fasting Explained

Intermittent Fasting comes in many shapes and sizes. I've written a book on the 5:2 method which is about eating normally 5 days a week and eating 500 calories on two separate days. This is the 16:8 method and as I mentioned this squeezes the eating window down to 8 hours and stretches the fasting period to 16 hours. So if you follow a 16-8 fast you will probably skip breakfast and have a large lunch at 12pm, then eat until 8pm, and then fast through the night and the next morning:

- Breakfast 12pm
- Lunch 4pm
- Dinner 7pm

We will be eating from a new meal plan which is designed for you to add and subtract foods. We also want to limit sugar and cut out all refined carbs such as cakes. All these fatty unhealthy foods are doing is adding to the work you need to do to burn them off. However we won't be living like monks and Sunday's are our cheat day, in that we can have a cheat meal and relax the hours of eating.

Instead we will be eating high protein foods and highly nutritious vegetables and fruits.

Liquids

Water is our friend and provides us with many benefits including: can help control calories, helps energize muscles, and helps keep skin looking great. I would try to lower coffee and tea consumption to around 2-3 cups day and get that down to 2 over the course of 2 weeks. I personally love my coffee with milk and 1 sugar and I don't want to cut that out so I have one day.

I would avoid sugary drinks as this will interfere with spiking insulin. We want this effect to be unadulterated. I would stick to water until you reach 12PM.

So without further ado let's begin.

4. Week 1 Workout

Monday - Back and Biceps

Week one begins - let's go.

Walk: 30 Minutes of cardio before breakfast. We want to burn fat before anything else and get the body prepared for the day.

Weights: I would do this around 4-6 when you're strongest. Or straight after work before dinner.

Round 1

The weights should be light enough to reach the 15-18 mark. 45 second between sets.

Exercise	Sets/Reps
CHIN-UP	1-2 sets of 15 reps (warm-up); 4 sets to failure
Superset	
BARBELL CURL	4 sets of 18-15 reps

If you cannot do many (or any) Chin-Ups, then stand on a stool to support some of your body weight. Hang down, and do the Chin-Up, pulling as hard as you can to pull up to the bar, and supporting as little of your weight on one foot.

Superset the Chin-Ups with the Barbell Curls- do one Chin-Up set, then a Barbell set, then repeat until finished.

Round 2

Increase the weight little by little with each set.

Exercise	Sets/Reps
WIDE-GRIP REAR PULL-UP	3 sets of 20, 18, 15 reps
Superset	
DUMBBELL ALTERNATE BICEP CURL	3 sets of 20-15 reps

Same as above if you cannot do many (or any) Pull-Ups.

Superset the Pull-Up sets with the Dumbbell Biceps Curls.

Round 3

Increase the weight little by little with each set.

Exercise	Sets/Reps
T-BAR ROW	3 sets of 20, 16, 12 reps
Superset	
INCLINE DUMBBELL REVERSE CURL	3 sets of 20-12 rep

Superset the Rows with the Dumbbell Reverse Curls. Reverse Curl means that your hands are facing away as you flex your elbow.

Nutrition

Upon Waking:

Have a long glass of warm water with lemon - either fresh lemon or pure lemon dripped in.

12 P.M - Breakfast - Meal One

- 1 x multivitamin
- 2 Whole Eggs Scrambled
- Mixed with Green beans cut up

NUTRITION FACTS

Calories: 409   Fat: 17.6 g   Carbs: 20.6 g   Protein: 16.3 g

4 P.M - Lunch - Meal Two

- Chicken Breast - With parsley, and bell peppers sliced up
- Vegetables - 1-2 cups

NUTRITION FACTS

Calories: 318   Fat: 15g   Carbs: 15g   Protein: 24g

7 PM - Dinner - Meal Three

- Tuna Steak
- Rocket and sliced Red Peppers
- Medium Sweet Potato

NUTRITION FACTS

Calories: 456   Fat: 17g Carbs: 29g   Protein: 28g

The Total Protein intake is 68.3 grams of protein. I would have 1 scoop of protein - 25grams - after your workout making a grand total of 93.3.

Notice how the carbs are minimal - except after your training. You can have carbs then, then stick with veg and fruit.

Tuesday - Abs/Cardio + Nutrition

Upon Waking:

Have a long glass of warm water with lemon - either fresh lemon or pure lemon dripped in.

Before Breakfast: These can be done later in the day

3 sets- 20 Crunches each set

3 sets- 25 Standing Twists each direction

3 sets- 20 Side-Lying Leg Lifts each direction

Run: Again, do this later in the day, at least after the first meal.

25-minute run (remember to warm up and down)

Include: 1 x Sprint in the run for 10 seconds.

Try to walk as much as possible, later on to from work or to a further station etc.

12 P.M - Breakfast - Meal One

- 1 x multivitamin
- 1 x Whey Protein shake - with peanut butter and a banana
- 1 30gram x Bowl of Granola

NUTRITION FACTS

Calories: 561   Fat: 30.4 g   Carbs: 26.2 g   Protein: 28 g

4 P.M - Lunch - Meal Two

- 1 x Medium sized Tuna Steak
- 1 x Cup Vegetables/salad

NUTRITION FACTS

Calories: 471   Fat: 33.2 g   Carbs: 17 g   Protein: 27

7 P.M - Dinner - Meal Three

- 2 Large Eggs Omelette with chopped green beans
- 2 Rice Cakes
- 1 x Peach

NUTRITION FACTS

Calories: 349   Fat: 14 g Carb: 25 g   Protein: 16 g

The Total Protein intake is 71 grams of protein. I would have 1 scoops of protein plus after your workout making a grand total of 96.

Wednesday - Chest and Triceps

Walk: 30 Minute brisk walk before breakfast - again breakfast is ideal.

Weights- Mid-afternoon is best.

Round 1

Increase the weight little by little with each set. 45 second break between sets.

Exercise	Sets/Reps
BARBELL BENCH PRESS - MEDIUM GRIP	1-2 sets of 15 reps (warm-up); 5 sets of 20, 18, 15, 15, 12 reps
Superset	
LYING TRICEPS PRESS	4 sets of 20, 18, 16, 16, reps

Superset the Bench Press and Triceps Press

Round 2

Increase the weight little by little with each set.

Exercise	Sets/Reps
BARBELL INCLINE BENCH PRESS	3 sets of 20, 18, 16 reps
Superset	
TRICEPS PUSHDOWN	3 sets of 20, 18, 16 reps

Superset the Incline Bench Press and Triceps Pushdown

Round 3

Increase the weight little by little with each set.

Exercise	Sets/Reps
DUMBBELL FLYS	3 sets of 20, 18, 16 reps
Superset	
CABLE ROPE OVERHEAD TRICEPS EXTENSION	3 sets of 20, 18, 18 reps

Superset the Flies and Triceps Overhead Pulls

You can add a set of Push Ups at the end

Nutrition

Upon Waking:

Have a long glass of warm water with lemon - either fresh lemon or pure lemon dripped in.

12 P.M - Breakfast - Meal One

- 1 x multivitamin
- 2 boiled eggs
- Porridge Oats 30gram serving with 1 tbsp. honey

NUTRITION FACTS

Calories: 409   Fat: 17.6 g   Carbs: 35.6 g   Protein: 20.3 g

4 P.M - Lunch - Meal Two

- Pork Chops 5 ounces- with cooked apple - cooked together
- Vegetables 1 cup

NUTRITION FACTS

Calories: 380   Fat: 18.2 g   Carbs: 25 g   Protein: 28 g

7 P.M - Dinner - Meal Three

- Full-Fat Cottage Cheese
- 1 cup Cashews
- 1 Apple
- 1 Banana

NUTRITION FACTS

Calories: 556   Fat: 17 g Carb: 59 g   Protein: 28 g

The Total Protein intake is 76.3 grams of protein. I would have 1 scoop of protein after your workout making a grand total of 101.3.

Thursday - Abs/Cardio + Nutrition

Upon Waking:

Have a long glass of warm water with lemon - either fresh lemon or pure lemon dripped in.

Run: 30-minute run. I'd like you to get in a good 30-minute walk at the end of the day.

After work:

3 sets of 30 Twists each side

3 set of Side Bends each side- if too easy, add a 5-10 pound dumbbell

4 sets of Hold plank – 30 seconds each

12 P.M - Breakfast - Meal One

- 1 x multivitamin
- 2 Whole Eggs Scrambled
- Mixed with Green beans cut up

NUTRITION FACTS

Calories: 409   Fat: 17.6 g   Carbs: 20.6 g   Protein: 16.3 g

4 P.M - Lunch - Meal Two

- Chicken Breast - With parsley, and bell peppers sliced up
- Steamed Broccoli

NUTRITION FACTS

Calories: 318   Fat: 15g   Carbs: 15g   Protein: 24g

7 PM - Dinner - Meal Three

- Tuna Steak
- Cucumber, tomatoes, Wild Rocket and Celery chunks

NUTRITION FACTS

Calories: 376   Fat: 17g   Carbs: 9g   Protein: 27g

The Total Protein intake is 67.3 grams of protein. I would have 1 scoop of protein - 25grams - after your workout making a grand total of 92.3.

Notice how the carbs are minimal - except after your training. You can have carbs then, then stick with veg and fruit.

Friday - Legs and Calves

Walk: 25-minute walk early to work, or before work round the block – it's leg day and so don't need to do anything too hard.

Round 1

I would certainly do this work out after work, amongst your feeding time so you have energy to train and can replace energy. Warm up thoroughly. Increase the weight little by little with each set.

Exercise	Sets/Reps
BARBELL SQUAT	2 warm up light sets, 4 sets of 20, 18, 16 reps
STANDING LEG CURL	3 sets of 20, 18, 16 reps
SMITH MACHINE LEG PRESS	3 sets of 15 reps

Do the Barbell Squat separately, and Superset the Standing Leg Curl and Leg Press

Round 2

Increase the weight little by little with each set.

Exercise	Sets/Reps
DEADLIFT	3 sets of 18, 18, 18 reps
LEG EXTENSIONS	3 sets of 20, 18, 16 reps
LEG CURLS	3 sets of 20 reps

Do the Deadlift separately, and Superset the Leg Extensions and Leg Curls

Round 3

Increase the weight little by little with each set.

Exercise	Sets/Reps
STANDING CALF RAISES	3 sets of 20, 18, 16 reps
Superset	
SEATED CALF RAISE	3 sets of 20-15 reps

Nutrition

Upon Waking:

Have a long glass of warm water with lemon - either fresh lemon or pure lemon dripped in.

12 P.M - Breakfast - Meal One

- 1 x multivitamin
- 1 x Whey Protein shake - with peanut butter and a banana
- 1 30gram x Bowl of Granola

NUTRITION FACTS

Calories: 561   Fat: 30.4 g   Carbs: 26.2 g   Protein: 28 g

4 P.M - Lunch - Meal Two

- Greek Yogurt - High Protein
- 1 x Sliced Peach
- 2 cups Cashews

NUTRITION FACTS

Calories: 752   Fat: 34 g   Carb: 18 g   Protein: 52 g

7 P.M - Dinner - Meal Three

- 1 x Medium sized Tuna Steak
- 1 x Cup Vegetables/salad
- 1 Medium sized Baked Potato

NUTRITION FACTS

Calories: 571   Fat: 33.2 g   Carbs: 80 g   Protein: 33 g

I've given you a huge carb dinner here after the leg workout and this will replenish your energy. Add a dab of butter too. The Total Protein intake is 113 grams of protein. I would have 1 scoops of protein plus after your workout making a grand total of 138.

Saturday - Abs/Cardio + Nutrition

Upon Waking:

Have a long glass of warm water with lemon - either fresh lemon or pure lemon dripped in.

Before Breakfast: - Ab Blast

20 x Crunches

25 x Twists

15 x sit-ups

20 x Crunches

25 x Twists

15 x sit-ups

20 x Crunches

25 x Twists

15 x sit-ups

Run: 30 minute run - during the morning.

12 P.M - Breakfast - Meal One

- 1 x multivitamin
- 1 Whole Egg
- 1 piece of salmon
- Oats 1/4 cup with 1 tbsp. honey

NUTRITION FACTS

Calories: 561   Fat: 30.4 g   Carbs: 20.2 g   Protein: 26.1 g

4 P.M - Lunch - Meal Two

- High Protein Frozen Yogurt
- Cashews 2 ounces
- 1 Apple

NUTRITION FACTS

Calories: 356   Fat: 17 g Carb: 9 g   Protein: 26 g

7 P.M - Dinner - Meal Four

- Pork Chops 5 ounces- with cooked apple - cooked together
- Vegetables 1 cup

NUTRITION FACTS

Calories: 380   Fat: 18.2 g   Carbs: 25 g   Protein: 28 g

The Total Protein intake is 80.1 grams of protein. I would have 1 scoop of protein after your workout making a grand total of 105.1.

Sunday - Rest

So we've made it to our rest day - well done for an epic week 1 of workouts! You should be feeling good, a little achy maybe, but you got through it. Did you miss any workouts? If so, it doesn't matter, let's go one better this coming week. It's about progression.

So today is all about chilling, eating well, having your cheat meal - which is anything of your choice. Also it's Sunday so you don't need to follow the strict eating times if you want a break. Not that it should ever feel a chore, but having breakfast at the old breakfast time never hurt anyone on a Sunday.

Upon Waking:

Have a long glass of warm water with lemon - either fresh lemon or pure lemon dripped in.

Breakfast - Meal One

- 1 x multivitamin
- 3 x scrambled eggs - with spinach
- 1 30gram x Bowl of Granola

NUTRITION FACTS

Calories: 561   Fat: 30.4 g   Carbs: 26.2 g   Protein: 26 g

Lunch - Meal Two

CHEAT MEAL - whatever you fancy!

7 P.M - Dinner - Meal Three

- 1 Cup x Full-Fat Cottage Cheese
- 1 x blob of peanut butter mixed in

NUTRITION FACTS

Calories: 371   Fat: 27 g Carb: 9 g   Protein: 24 g

For future cheat meals, I'm not going into your exact macros here. Eat well and enjoy yourself until tomorrow.

5. Week 2 Workout

Monday - Cardio

Week 2 is all about cardio. So we allow the body time to recover from the weight training and now we focus on burning fat. We want to rev up your metabolism so we will be doing cardio in the morning before breakfast and we will making use of a pedometer that almost every smart phone has.

I want you to be doing 6000 steps a day this week on top of your cardio. That roughly equates to 1 hour of walking. There is usually a step counter built into your smart phone and you can do this without even thinking. Just work this into getting to and from work and a walk on your lunch break and it'll be done without even trying.

To maximize the benefits of a cardio workout, you have to elevate your heart rate and keep it elevated for at least 20 consecutive minutes. You will want to monitor your heart rate during the workouts. You will also want to move quickly from one exercise to the next, and keep the breaks short so your heart rate stays elevated This will improve your heart and lung function, and actually begin to grow new blood vessels into your muscles.

IF YOU ARE OVER 40 YEARS OLD, OR HAVE A HISTORY OF HEART DISEASE, THEN YOU SHOULD BE MEDICALLY CLEARED BY YOUR PHYSICIAN BEFORE STARTING ANY CARDIO EXERCISE PROGRAM.

The formula for your target heart rate is based on your theoretical maximum heart rate. Subtract your age from 220.

This is your maximum heart rate. Your target rate is 60-80% of the maximum.

For example- if you are 20, your maximum heart rate is 200. The target rate is 120-160. So you need to exercise at a level that raises your heart rate to this range and keeps it there for at least 20 minutes.

Here is a great routine for HIIT - High Intensity Interval Training. Let's ramp up the fat burning and get down to it!

Cardio

Do this 3 times. Go!

Three circuits: 10 reps per exercise. No rests.

Round One:

- **Burpees**
- **Press-ups**
- **Jumping Jacks**

- **Skipping rope: 3 minutes**

Rest 1 minute

Three circuits: 15 reps per exercise. No rest

Round Two:

- **Walking Lunges with kettlebell exchange underneath leg**
- **Star jumps**
- **High knees running on the spot**

- **Skipping rope: 3 minutes**

Rest 1 minute

Three circuits: 25 reps per exercise. No rest.

Round Three:

- **Pullups**
- **Box Jumps**
- **Star jumps**

- **Skipping rope: 3 minutes**

Rest 1 minute

Three circuits: 30 reps per move. No Rest

Round Four:

- **Alternate Side Lunges**
- **Dips**
- **Shadow boxing**

Nutrition

Upon Waking:

Have a long glass of warm water with lemon - either fresh lemon or pure lemon dripped in.

12 P.M - Breakfast - Meal One

- 1 x multivitamin
- 2 Whole Eggs Scrambled

- Mixed with Green beans cut up

NUTRITION FACTS

Calories: 409   Fat: 17.6 g   Carbs: 20.6 g   Protein: 16.3 g

4 P.M - Lunch - Meal Two

- 1 Can of Tuna Steak
- Red bell peppers, and low fat Coleslaw

NUTRITION FACTS

Calories: 386   Fat: 17g Carbs: 17g   Protein: 27g

7 P.M - Dinner - Meal Three

- Chicken Breast - With parsley, and bell peppers sliced up
- Peas and Carrots

NUTRITION FACTS

Calories: 318   Fat: 15g   Carbs: 15g   Protein: 24g

The Total Protein intake is 67.3 grams of protein. I would have 1 scoop of protein - 25grams - after your workout making a grand total of 92.3.

Notice how the carbs are minimal - except after your training. You can have carbs then, then stick with veg and fruit.

Tuesday - Cardio

Before Breakfast:

Very simple, do about 5 minutes of stretches and then go for an early 30 minute run - outside or use the running machine in a gym.

Be sure to warm down.

Plus, remember your walking today - as much as you can.

Nutrition

Upon Waking:

Have a long glass of warm water with lemon - either fresh lemon or pure lemon dripped in.

12 P.M - Breakfast - Meal One

- 1 x multivitamin
- 1 x Whey Protein shake - with peanut butter and a banana
- 1 30gram x Bowl of Granola

NUTRITION FACTS

Calories: 561   Fat: 30.4 g   Carbs: 26.2 g   Protein: 28 g

4 P.M - Lunch - Meal Two

- 1 x Medium sized Tuna Steak
- 1 x Cup Vegetables/salad

NUTRITION FACTS

Calories: 471   Fat: 33.2 g   Carbs: 17 g   Protein: 27 g

7 PM - Dinner - Meal Three

- Tuna Steak
- Rocket and sliced Red Peppers
- Medium Sweet Potato

NUTRITION FACTS

Calories: 456   Fat: 17g Carbs: 29g   Protein: 28g

The Total Protein intake is 83 grams of protein. I would have 1 scoops of protein plus after your workout making a grand total of 108.

Wednesday - Cardio

Cardio

Do this 3 times. Go!

Three circuits: 10 reps per exercise. No rests.

Round One:

- **Burpees**
- **Press-ups**
- **Jumping Jacks**

- **Skipping rope: 3 minutes**

Rest 1 minute

Three circuits: 15 reps per exercise. No rest

Round Two:

- **Walking Lunges with kettlebell exchange underneath leg**
- **Star jumps**
- **High knees running on the spot**

- **Skipping rope: 3 minutes**

Rest 1 minute

Three circuits: 25 reps per exercise. No rest.

Round Three:

- **Pullups**
- **Box Jumps**
- **Star jumps**

- **Skipping rope: 3 minutes**

Rest 1 minute

Three circuits: 30 reps per move. No Rest

Round Four:

- **Alternate Side Lunges**
- **Dips**
- **Shadow boxing**

Nutrition

Upon Waking:

Have a long glass of warm water with lemon - either fresh lemon or pure lemon dripped in.

12 P.M - Breakfast - Meal One

- 1 x multivitamin
- 2 boiled eggs
- Porridge Oats 30gram serving with 1 tbsp. honey

NUTRITION FACTS

Calories: 409   Fat: 17.6 g   Carbs: 35.6 g   Protein: 20.3 g

4 P.M - Lunch - Meal Two

- Full-Fat Cottage Cheese
- 1 cup Cashews
- 1 Pear
- 1 Banana

NUTRITION FACTS

Calories: 566   Fat: 17 g Carb: 59 g   Protein: 28 g

7 P.M - Dinner - Meal Three

- Pork Chops 5 ounces- with cooked apple - cooked together
- Vegetables 1 cup

NUTRITION FACTS

Calories: 380   Fat: 18.2 g   Carbs: 25 g   Protein: 28 g

The Total Protein intake is 76.3 grams of protein. I would have 1 scoop of protein after your workout making a grand total of 101.3.

Thursday - Cardio

Before Breakfast:

Very simple, do about 5 minutes of stretches and then go for an early 25 minutes of spinning or a bike ride - outside or use the running machine in a gym.

Or just stick to the pavement and do a 30 minute run.

Be sure to warm down.

Nutrition

Upon Waking:

Have a long glass of warm water with lemon - either fresh lemon or pure lemon dripped in.

12 P.M - Breakfast - Meal One

- 1 x multivitamin
- 1 x Whey Protein shake - with peanut butter and a banana
- 1 30gram x Bowl of Granola

NUTRITION FACTS

Calories: 561   Fat: 30.4 g   Carbs: 26.2 g   Protein: 28 g

4 P.M Lunch - Meal Two

- 1 x can of Tuna Steak
- Rocket and Beetroot

NUTRITION FACTS

Calories: 471   Fat: 33.2 g   Carbs: 17 g   Protein: 27 g

7 P.M Dinner - Meal Three

- Chicken Breast - With parsley, and bell peppers sliced up
- Steamed Broccoli

NUTRITION FACTS

Calories: 318   Fat: 15g   Carbs: 15g   Protein: 24g

The Total Protein intake is 79 grams of protein. I would have 1 scoops of protein plus after your workout making a grand total of 104.

Friday - Cardio

Cardio

Do this 3 times. Go!

Three circuits: 10 reps per exercise. No rests.

Round One:

- **Burpees**
- **Press-ups**
- **Jumping Jacks**

- **Skipping rope: 3 minutes**

Rest 1 minute

Three circuits: 15 reps per exercise. No rest

Round Two:

- **Walking Lunges with kettlebell exchange underneath leg**
- **Star jumps**
- **High knees running on the spot**

- **Skipping rope: 3 minutes**

Rest 1 minute

Three circuits: 25 reps per exercise. No rest.

Round Three:

- **Pullups**
- **Box Jumps**
- **Star jumps**

- **Skipping rope: 3 minutes**

Rest 1 minute

Three circuits: 30 reps per move. No Rest

Round Four:

- **Alternate Side Lunges**
- **Dips**
- **Shadow boxing**

Nutrition

Upon Waking:

Have a long glass of warm water with lemon - either fresh lemon or pure lemon dripped in.

12 P.M - Breakfast - Meal One

- 1 x multivitamin
- 2 Whole Eggs Scrambled
- Mixed with Green beans cut up

NUTRITION FACTS

Calories: 409   Fat: 17.6 g   Carbs: 20.6 g   Protein: 16.3 g

4 P.M Lunch - Meal Two

- 1 x Medium sized Tuna Steak
- 1 x Cup Vegetables/salad
- 1 Medium sized Baked Potato

NUTRITION FACTS

Calories: 571   Fat: 33.2 g   Carbs: 80 g   Protein: 33 g

7 P.M - Dinner - Meal Three

- Chicken Breast - With parsley, and bell peppers sliced up
- Sprouts - cooked and mashed - add pepper and soft cheese - mash up

NUTRITION FACTS

Calories: 418   Fat: 15g   Carbs: 28g   Protein: 29g

The Total Protein intake is 78.3 grams of protein. I would have 1 scoop of protein - 25grams - after your workout making a grand total of 103.3.

Saturday - Cardio

Before Breakfast

1 hour of swimming - or 1 x 45 minute insanity workout.

In terms of swimming I want to mix it up, this is also very low impact, your muscles could probably do with something relaxing. Try to put in lengths and keep moving.

Again warming up and cooling down is very important.

Nutrition

Upon Waking:

Have a long glass of warm water with lemon - either fresh lemon or pure lemon dripped in.

12 P.M - Breakfast - Meal One

- 1 x multivitamin
- 2 boiled eggs
- Porridge Oats 30gram serving with 1 tbsp. honey

NUTRITION FACTS

Calories: 409   Fat: 17.6 g   Carbs: 35.6 g   Protein: 20.3 g

4 P.M - Lunch - Meal Two

- Full-Fat Cottage Cheese
- 1 cups Cashews
- 1 Apple

NUTRITION FACTS

Calories: 356   Fat: 17 g Carb: 9 g   Protein: 26 g

7 P.M - Dinner - Meal Three

- Pork Chops 5 ounces- with cooked apple - cooked together
- Vegetables 1 cup

NUTRITION FACTS

Calories: 380   Fat: 18.2 g   Carbs: 25 g   Protein: 28 g

The Total Protein intake is 74.3 grams of protein. I would have 1 scoop of protein after your workout making a grand total of 99.3.

Sunday - Rest and Nutrition

We've reached Week 2 of the workout! You're probably starting to notice the changes on your stomach becoming a set of abs, and the muscles on your arms and legs stating to form. But for now, let's give them a much needed breather, for today is your break day. After all those cardio workouts, your heart certainly needs it.

Like last week, you're free to have your cheat meal and lax eating times.

Upon Waking:

Have a long glass of warm water with lemon - either fresh lemon or pure lemon dripped in.

Breakfast - Meal One

- 1 x multivitamin
- 3 x scrambled eggs - with spinach
- 1 30gram x Bowl of Granola

NUTRITION FACTS

Calories: 561   Fat: 30.4 g   Carbs: 26.2 g   Protein: 26 g

Lunch - Meal Two

CHEAT MEAL - whatever you fancy!

7 P.M - Dinner - Meal Three

- 1 Cup x Full-Fat Cottage Cheese
- 1 x blob of peanut butter mixed in

NUTRITION FACTS

Calories: 371   Fat: 27 g Carb: 9 g   Protein: 24 g

6. Week 3 Workout

Monday

Warm-up, or meditate, by sitting cross-legged on the floor. Make sure your back is straight and your hands are relaxed on your lap. Relax, close your eyes, and slowly breath in and out as you bend your body left and right for 15 breaths. Do this after your wake-up water but before breakfast.

Yoga

Every day this week is a yoga day, and will be focused on comfortable stretches. Make sure these movements flow, and hold the positions for at least three breaths for each. Once you are done, switch back to the warm-up cross-leg position to rest. Also, be sure to get a Yoga mat, or at least do this on a comfortable floor.

I'll explain how to do the poses first time around. Breather is like a Rep but it lasts as long as you can hold an inhale and exhale. If you're still having trouble or are not sure if you're doing the stretches right, try a Google search.

Cow and Cat pose – Stand on all fours. Cow pose arcs your back down, press shoulders away from head. Cat pose rounds your back, lowers your head, lifts belly and you try to see your thighs. Switch from Cow to Cat 5 times.

Downward Dog pose – Still on all fours, arc your back up to form a triangle or inverted V. Try to push your knees down and then back up. Hold, then rise and repeat 5 times.

Extended Side Angle – Lead with your right leg in a lunge, turn heel 45 degrees. With your right hand lose, reach and extend with your right over your head, making a straight line from heel to fingers. Hold for the usual 3 breaths, and then switch once to lean on your left leg.

Child's Pose – kneel down, lay back and face down as your hands stretch out. Keep your chest as close to your legs as possible. Simply relax and breath.

Rest break of 1 minute

Downward Dog pose – repeat 5 times

Extended Side Angle – start left, then right. Hold for 3 breathers each.
Cow and Cat pose – switch 5 times

Child Pose – hold for 5 breathers.

Rest for 5 minutes, end session.

Nutrition

For the duration of this week, we'll be eating less protein. That means no meats unless it's a cheat meal, and that you'll have to eat a lot more fruits and veggies.

Upon Waking:

Have a long glass of warm water with lemon - either fresh lemon or pure lemon dripped in.

12 PM Breakfast – Meal One

- 1 x multivitamin
- An Orange
- Mixed with Green beans cut up

NUTRITION FACTS

Calories: 289   Fat: 4.4 g   Carbs: 34 g   Protein: 5.3 g

4 PM Lunch – Meal Two

- Fruit Salad Cup (Peach, Pear, Apricot, Pineapple, Cherry)
- Frozen Yogurt

NUTRITION FACTS
Calories: 275 Fat: 2.1g Carbs: 49.5g Protein: 21.3g

7 PM Dinner – Meal Three

- Smooth Peanut-Butter Sandwich (2 cups, 2 slices of bread)
- Apple

NUTRITION FACTS

Calories: 442 Fat: 18.3g Carbs: 60.3g Protein: 15.8

Total protein gain is 42.4 g. However, this week is about stretching muscles then building them. You need more protein when you work out because it converts to muscle. If you earn too much protein and don't work it off, you'll instead get fat, which is not what we want. That's why for your diet this week, abstain on eating meat and cups of protein.

Tuesday

Meditate cross-legged style for 15 breaths. Do this after the wake-up water but before breakfast.

Yoga

Mountain Pose – stand tall, feet together, shoulders relaxed. Each one of your 3 breathers, try to extend higher.

Tree Pose – arms raised then prayer, balance on one leg. Switch to next leg after 15 breathers.

Warrior Pose – stand 3-4 feet apart, bend forward leg 90 degrees, stay for 1 minute or 15 breathers before switching.

Pidgeon Pose – from a push-up position, kneel your left knee near shoulder. Lower down to forearms, allow right foot to be placed perfectly against the floor. Hold for 15 breathers and then switch legs.

Rest for 1 minute.

Pidgeon Pose – 15 breathers for each leg.

Tree Pose – 15 breathers for each leg.

Mountain Pose – 3 breathers, reach higher each time
Warrior Pose – 15 breathers for each leg.

Rest for 5 minutes, end session.

Nutrition

Upon Waking:

Have a long glass of warm water with lemon - either fresh lemon or pure lemon dripped in.

12 PM Breakfast – Meal One

- 1 x multivitamin
- An Orange
- Mixed with Green beans cut up

NUTRITION FACTS

Calories: 289   Fat: 4.4 g   Carbs: 34 g   Protein: 5.3 g

4 PM Lunch – Meal Two

- Fruit Salad Cup (Peach, Pear, Apricot, Pineapple, Cherry)
- Frozen Yogurt

NUTRITION FACTS
Calories: 275 Fat: 2.1g Carbs: 49.5g Protein: 21.3g

7 PM Dinner – Meal Three

- Smooth Peanut-Butter Sandwich (2 cups, 2 slices of bread)
- Apple

NUTRITION FACTS

Calories: 442 Fat: 18.3g Carbs: 60.3g Protein: 15.8

Total protein gain is 42.4 g.

Wednesday

Meditate cross-legged style for 15 breaths. Do this after wake-up water but before breakfast.

Yoga

Bridge Pose – lie on floor on your back with bent knees and arms flat on floor. Lift hips with feet in place as you exhale. Hold for 1 minute or 15 breathers.

Cobra Pose – lie face first on the floor, thumbs under shoulders and top of the feet on the floor slide. Push your body through thumb and index finger to rise upper body. Rinse and repeat 5 times.

Crow Pose – From Downward Dog position, move feet forward until the knees are touching the arms. Bend your elbows, stand on your toes, and rest knees against arms. Hold position for 10 breathers.

Seated Twist – Sit down with legs extended. Cross right foot over outside of left thigh and bend right knee with it pointed to ceiling. Place left elbow outside of right knee and right hand behind you on the floor. Twist your abdomen as far as you can, with your butt firm on the floor. Hold for a minute or 15 breathers before switching to the other side.

Rest for 1 minute.

Seated Twist – 15 breathers for each side.

Cobra Pose – Rise and fall 5 times.

Bridge Pose – Hold for 15 breathers.

Crow Pose – Hold for 10 breathers.

Nutrition

Upon Waking:

Have a long glass of warm water with lemon - either fresh lemon or pure lemon dripped in.

12 PM Breakfast – Meal One

- 1 x multivitamin
- An Orange
- Porridge Oats 30gram serving with 1 tbsp. honey

NUTRITION FACTS

Calories: 427 Fat: 8.2g   Carbs: 50.2 g Protein: 8.9 g

4 P.M - Lunch - Meal Two

- Full-Fat Cottage Cheese
- 1 cups Cashews
- 1 Apple

NUTRITION FACTS

Calories: 356   Fat: 17 g Carb: 9 g   Protein: 26 g

7 PM Dinner – Meal Three

- Canned Tomato Soup
- Full-Fat Cottage Cheese
- Saltine Crackers

NUTRITION FACTS

Calories: 292 Fat: 7.2g Carb: 41g Protein: 18.7g

Total protein gain is 53.6g. Remember not to eat any protein cups this week.

Thursday

Meditate cross-legged style for 15 breaths. Do this after wake-up water but before breakfast.

Yoga

Again, flow and hold the positions for three breaths for each. Once you are done, switch back to the warm-up cross-leg position to rest.

Cow and Cat pose – Switch from Cow to Cat 5 times.
Downward Dog pose – Hold and then switch 5 times
Extended Side Angle – switch legs after 3 breathers
Child's Pose – hold for 5 breaths

Rest break of 1 minute

Downward Dog pose – repeat 5 times

Extended Side Angle – switch legs after 3 breathers
Cow and Cat pose – switch 5 times

Child Pose – hold for 5 breathers.

Rest for 5 minutes, end session.

Nutrition

Upon Waking:

Have a long glass of warm water with lemon - either fresh lemon or pure lemon dripped in.

12 PM Breakfast – Meal One

- 1 x multivitamin
- An Orange
- Mixed with Green beans cut up

NUTRITION FACTS

Calories: 289   Fat: 4.4 g   Carbs: 34 g   Protein: 5.3 g

4 PM Lunch – Meal Two

- Fruit Salad Cup (Peach, Pear, Apricot, Pineapple, Cherry)
- Frozen Yogurt

NUTRITION FACTS
Calories: 275 Fat: 2.1 g Carbs: 49.5g Protein: 21.3g

7 PM Dinner – Meal Three

- Smooth Peanut-Butter Sandwich (2 cups, 2 slices of bread)
- Apple

NUTRITION FACTS

Calories: 442 Fat: 18.3g Carbs: 60.3g Protein: 15.8

Total protein gain is 42.4g.

Friday

Meditate cross-legged style for 15 breaths. Do this after wake-up water but before breakfast.

Seated Twist – 15 breathers for each side.
Pidgeon Pose – 15 breathers per leg.
Downward Dog – repeat 5 times.
Child Pose – hold for 5 breathers.

Rest for 1 minute.

Pidgeon Pose – 15 breathers per leg.
Downward Dog – repeat 5 times.
Seated Twist – 15 breathers for each side.

Child Pose – hold for 5 breathers.

Rest for 5 minutes. End session.

Nutrition

Upon Waking:

Have a long glass of warm water with lemon - either fresh lemon or pure lemon dripped in.

12 PM Breakfast – Meal One

- 1 x multivitamin
- An Orange
- Porridge Oats 30gram serving with 1 tbsp. honey

NUTRITION FACTS

Calories: 427 Fat: 8.2 g   Carbs: 50.2 g Protein: 8.9 g

4 PM Lunch – Meal Two

- Full-Fat Cottage Cheese
- 1 cups Cashews
- 1 Apple

NUTRITION FACTS

Calories: 356   Fat: 17 g Carb: 9 g   Protein: 26 g

7 PM Dinner – Meal Three

- Smooth Peanut-Butter Sandwich (2 cups, 2 slices of bread)
- Apple

NUTRITION FACTS

Calories: 442 Fat: 18.3g Carbs: 60.3g Protein: 15.8

Total protein gain is 50.7g

Saturday

Tree Pose – 15 breathers for each leg.

Extended Side Angle – switch legs between 3 breathers
Mountain Pose – 3 breathers, reach higher each time

Warrior Pose – 15 breathers for each leg.

Rest for 1 minute.

Mountain Pose – 3 breathers, reach higher each time.
Warrior Pose – 15 breathers for each leg.

Extended Side Angle – switch legs between 3 breathers.

Tree Pose – 15 breathers for each leg

Rest for 5 minutes. End session.

Nutrition

Upon Waking:

Have a long glass of warm water with lemon - either fresh lemon or pure lemon dripped in.

12 P.M - Breakfast - Meal One

- 1 x multivitamin
- An Orange
- Porridge Oats 30gram serving with 1 tbsp. honey

NUTRITION FACTS

Calories: 427 Fat: 8.2 g   Carbs: 50.2 g Protein: 8.9 g

4 P.M - Lunch - Meal Two

- Full-Fat Cottage Cheese
- 1 cups Cashews
- 1 Apple

NUTRITION FACTS

Calories: 356   Fat: 17 g Carb: 9 g   Protein: 26 g

7 PM Dinner

- Canned Tomato Soup
- Full-Fat Cottage Cheese
- Saltine Crackers

NUTRITION FACTS

Calories: 292 Fat: 7.2g Carb: 41g Protein: 18.7g

Total protein gain is 53.6g

Sunday - Rest and Nutrition

So we have reached the end of week 3. I hope you feel tired, and achy but more importantly feel like you're making progress, slimming down, looking great and feeling great. You are now half-way there, now!

For being so dedicated I've given you two cheat meals today, they can actually be wherever you want - Breakfast/Dinner, Breakfast/Lunch etc. It's important for us to kick back and enjoy our hard work and to indulge in the odd cake.

Today is all about chilling, eating well, having your cheat meal - which is anything of your choice. I've also added a sneaky scoop of ice cream with your protein shake for doing so well.

Of course, come tomorrow of this workout you'll need to step up and work just as hard as the first three weeks. But for now, you earned yourself a reward to relax. You don't have to stick to the regimented Intermittent Fasting rules, so today you can take a break.

Upon Waking:

Have a long glass of warm water with lemon - either fresh lemon or pure lemon dripped in.

Breakfast - Meal One

- 1 x multivitamin
- 1 x Whey Protein shake - with peanut butter, a banana and a scoop of ice cream
- 1 30gram x Bowl of Granola

NUTRITION FACTS

Calories: 561   Fat: 35.4 g   Carbs: 26.2 g   Protein: 30 g

Lunch - Meal Two

CHEAT MEAL - whatever you fancy!

Dinner - Meal

CHEAT MEAL - whatever you fancy!

7. Week 4 Workout

It's back to weights again for your 4th week of intermittent fasting. You might notice that the workout is similar and sketched out the same as Week 1. The major difference is that each work-out session requires longer reps, now that your body is used to it.

Monday - Back and Biceps

Once more with feeling – weights go!

Walk: 30 Minutes of cardio before breakfast. Burn the fat and get the body ready.

Weights: I would do this around 4-6 when you're strongest. Or straight after work before dinner.

Round 1

Increase the weight little by little with each set. 45 second between sets.

Exercise	Sets/Reps
CHIN-UP	1-2 sets of 20 reps (warm-up); 3 sets of 15, 12, 10 reps
Superset	
BARBELL CURL	3 sets of 15-20 reps

Round 2

Increase the weight little by little with each set.

Exercise	Sets/Reps
WIDE-GRIP REAR PULL-UP	3 sets of 20, 15, 10 reps
Superset	
DUMBBELL ALTERNATE BICEP CURL	3 sets of 15-20 reps

Round 3

Increase the weight little by little with each set.

Exercise	Sets/Reps
T-BAR ROW	3 sets of 20, 15, 10 reps
Superset	
INCLINE DUMBBELL CURL	3 sets of 15-20 rep

Nutrition

Upon Waking:

Have a long glass of warm water with lemon - either fresh lemon or pure lemon dripped in.

12 P.M - Breakfast - Meal One

- 1 x multivitamin
- 2 Whole Eggs Scrambled
- Mixed with Green beans cut up

NUTRITION FACTS

Calories: 409   Fat: 17.6 g   Carbs: 20.6 g   Protein: 16.3 g

4 P.M - Lunch - Meal Two

- Chicken Breast - With parsley, and bell peppers sliced up
- Vegetables - 1-2 cups

NUTRITION FACTS

Calories: 318   Fat: 15g   Carbs: 15g   Protein: 24g

7 PM - Dinner - Meal Three

- Tuna Steak
- Rocket and sliced Red Peppers
- Medium Sweet Potato

NUTRITION FACTS

Calories: 456   Fat: 17g Carbs: 29g   Protein: 28g

Tuesday - Abs/Cardio + Nutrition

Upon Waking:

Have a long glass of warm water with lemon - either fresh lemon or pure lemon dripped in.

Before Breakfast:

40 x Crunches x 3

50 twists x 3 each side

Run: 30-minute run (remember to warm up and down) Try to walk as much as possible, later on to from work or to a further station etc.

Include 3 x sprints within the run

12 P.M - Breakfast - Meal One

- 1 x multivitamin
- 1 x Whey Protein shake - with peanut butter and a banana
- 1 30gram x Bowl of Granola

NUTRITION FACTS

Calories: 561   Fat: 30.4 g   Carbs: 26.2 g   Protein: 28 g

4 P.M - Lunch - Meal Two

- 1 x Medium sized Tuna Steak
- 1 x Cup Vegetables/salad

NUTRITION FACTS

Calories: 471   Fat: 33.2 g   Carbs: 17 g   Protein: 27 g

7 P.M - Dinner - Meal Three

- 2 Large Eggs Omelette with chopped green beans
- 2 Rice Cakes
- 1 x Peach

NUTRITION FACTS

Calories: 349   Fat: 14 g Carb: 25 g   Protein: 16 g

The Total Protein intake is 71 grams of protein. I would have 1 scoop of protein plus after your workout making a grand total of 96.

Wednesday - Chest and Triceps

Walk: 30 Minute brisk walk before breakfast - again breakfast is ideal.

Weights: As I said before breakfast or straight after work.

Round 1

Increase the weight little by little with each set. 45 second break between sets.

Exercise	Sets/Reps
BARBELL BENCH PRESS - MEDIUM GRIP	1-2 sets of 20 reps (warm-up); 3 sets of 30, 28, 25 reps
Superset	
LYING TRICEPS PRESS	3 sets of 30, 28, 24 reps

Round 2

Increase the weight little by little with each set.

Exercise	Sets/Reps
BARBELL INCLINE BENCH PRESS	3 sets of 30, 25, 22 reps
Superset	
TRICEPS PUSHDOWN	3 sets of 25, 23, 21, reps

Round 3

Increase the weight little by little with each set.

Exercise	Sets/Reps
DUMBBELL FLYES	3 sets of 30, 25, 22 reps
Superset	
CABLE ROPE OVERHEAD TRICEPS EXTENSION	3 sets of 30, 25, 22 reps

Nutrition

Upon Waking:

Have a long glass of warm water with lemon - either fresh lemon or pure lemon dripped in.

12 P.M - Breakfast - Meal One

- 1 x multivitamin
- 2 boiled eggs
- Porridge Oats 30gram serving with 1 tbsp. honey

NUTRITION FACTS

Calories: 409   Fat: 17.6 g   Carbs: 35.6 g   Protein: 20.3 g

4 P.M - Lunch - Meal Two

- Pork Chops 5 ounces- with cooked apple - cooked together
- Vegetables 1 cup

NUTRITION FACTS

Calories: 380   Fat: 18.2 g   Carbs: 25 g   Protein: 28 g

7 P.M - Dinner - Meal Three

- Full-Fat Cottage Cheese
- 1 cup Cashews
- 1 Apple
- 1 Banana

NUTRITION FACTS

Calories: 556   Fat: 17 g Carb: 59 g   Protein: 28 g

The Total Protein intake is 76.3 grams of protein. I would have 1 scoop of protein after your workout making a grand total of 101.3.

Thursday - Abs/Cardio + Nutrition

Upon Waking:

Have a long glass of warm water with lemon - either fresh lemon or pure lemon dripped in.

Run: 30-minute run before breakfast. I'd like you to get in a good 30-minute walk at the end of the day.

Include 3 x sprints within the run.

After work:

25 twists x 3 each side

Hold plank - 30 seconds x 3 (This helps strengthen your core body)

12 P.M - Breakfast - Meal One

- 1 x multivitamin
- 2 Whole Eggs Scrambled
- Mixed with Green beans cut up

NUTRITION FACTS

Calories: 409   Fat: 17.6 g   Carbs: 20.6 g   Protein: 16.3 g

4 P.M - Lunch - Meal Two

- Chicken Breast - With parsley, and bell peppers sliced up
- Steamed Broccoli

NUTRITION FACTS

Calories: 318   Fat: 15g   Carbs: 15g   Protein: 24g

7 PM - Dinner - Meal Three

- Tuna Steak
- Cucumber, tomatoes, Wild Rocket and Celery chunks

NUTRITION FACTS

Calories: 376   Fat: 17g Carbs: 9g   Protein: 27g

The Total Protein intake is 67.3 grams of protein. I would have 1 scoop of protein - 25grams - after your workout making a grand total of 92.3.

Notice how the carbs are minimal - except after your training. You can have carbs then, then stick with veg and fruit.

Friday - Legs and Calves

Walk: 25-minute walk early to work, or before work round the block - it's leg day and so need to do anything too hard.

Round 1

I would certainly do this work out after work, amongst your feeding time so you have energy to train and can replace energy. Warm up thoroughly. Increase the weight little by little with each set.

Exercise	Sets/Reps
BARBELL SQUAT	2 warm up light sets, 4 sets of 30, 25, 23, 20 reps
STANDING LEG CURL	3 sets of 30, 25, 22 reps
SMITH MACHINE LEG PRESS	3 sets of 30 reps

Round 2

Increase the weight little by little with each set.

Exercise	Sets/Reps
DEADLIFT	3 sets of 25, 22, 20 reps
LEG EXTENSIONS	3 sets of 30, 28, 25 reps
LEG CURLS	3 sets of 25 reps

Round 3

Increase the weight little by little with each set.

Exercise	Sets/Reps
STANDING CALF RAISES	3 sets of 30, 25, 25 reps
SEATED CALF RAISE	3 sets of 30-20 reps

Nutrition

Upon Waking:

Have a long glass of warm water with lemon - either fresh lemon or pure lemon dripped in.

12 P.M - Breakfast - Meal One

- 1 x multivitamin
- 1 x Whey Protein shake - with peanut butter and a banana
- 1 30gram x Bowl of Granola

NUTRITION FACTS

Calories: 561   Fat: 30.4 g   Carbs: 26.2 g   Protein: 28 g

4 P.M - Lunch - Meal Two

- Greek Yogurt - High Protein
- 1 x Sliced Peach
- 2 cups Cashews

NUTRITION FACTS

Calories: 752   Fat: 34 g Carb: 18 g   Protein: 52 g

7 P.M - Dinner - Meal Three

- 1 x Medium sized Tuna Steak
- 1 x Cup Vegetables/salad
- 1 Medium sized Baked Potato

NUTRITION FACTS

Calories: 571   Fat: 33.2 g   Carbs: 80 g   Protein: 33 g

I've given you a huge carb dinner here after the leg workout
and this will replenish your energy. Add a dab of butter too.
The Total Protein intake is 113 grams of protein. I would have 1
scoop of protein plus after your workout making a grand total
of 138.

Saturday - Abs/Cardio + Nutrition

Upon Waking:

Have a long glass of warm water with lemon - either fresh lemon or pure lemon dripped in.

Before Breakfast: - Ab Blast

20 x Crunches

25 x Twists

15 x sit-ups

20 x Crunches

25 x Twists

15 x sit-ups

20 x Crunches

25 x Twists

15 x sit-ups

Run: 30-minute run - during the morning.

Include 4 x sprints

12 P.M - Breakfast - Meal One

- 1 x multivitamin
- 1 Whole Egg
- 1 piece of salmon
- Oats 1/4 cup with 1 tbsp. honey

NUTRITION FACTS

Calories: 561   Fat: 30.4 g   Carbs: 20.2 g   Protein: 26.1 g

4 P.M - Lunch - Meal Two

- High Protein Frozen Yogurt
- Cashews 2 ounces
- 1 Apple

NUTRITION FACTS

Calories: 356   Fat: 17 g Carb: 9 g   Protein: 26 g

7 P.M - Dinner - Meal Four

- Pork Chops 5 ounces- with cooked apple - cooked together
- Vegetables 1 cup

NUTRITION FACTS

Calories: 380   Fat: 18.2 g   Carbs: 25 g   Protein: 28 g

The Total Protein intake is 80.1 grams of protein. I would have 1 scoop of protein after your workout making a grand total of 105.1.

Sunday - Rest

Another week, another well-earned rest. Feel free to have your cheat meal for lunch, again without worry about nutrition facts.

Upon Waking:

Have a long glass of warm water with lemon - either fresh lemon or pure lemon dripped in.

Breakfast - Meal One

- 1 x multivitamin
- 3 x scrambled eggs - with spinach
- 1 30gram x Bowl of Granola

NUTRITION FACTS

Calories: 561   Fat: 30.4 g   Carbs: 26.2 g   Protein: 26 g

Lunch - Meal Two

CHEAT MEAL - whatever you fancy!

7 P.M - Dinner - Meal Three

- 1 Cup x Full-Fat Cottage Cheese
- 1 x blob of peanut butter mixed in

NUTRITION FACTS

Calories: 371   Fat: 27 g Carb: 9 g   Protein: 24 g

8. Week 5 Workout

Monday - Cardio

Back to week 5 is cardio. Since we worked harder on weights, we're going to work harder on burning fat. On top of longer sets, this time you'll have to make 10000 steps a day.

<u>Cardio</u>

Do this 3 times. Go!

Three circuits: 10 reps per exercise. No rests.

Round One:

- **Burpees**
- **Press-ups**
- **Jumping Jacks**

- **Skipping rope: 5 minutes**

Rest 30 seconds -

Three circuits: 20 reps per exercise. No rest

Round Two:

- **Walking Lunges with kettlebell exchange underneath leg**
- **Star jumps**
- **High knees running on the spot**

- **Skipping rope: 5 minutes**

Rest 1 minute

Three circuits: 30 reps per exercise. No rest.

Round Three:

- **Pullups**
- **Box Jumps**
- **Star jumps**
- **Skipping rope: 5 minutes**

Rest 1 minute

Three circuits: 40 reps per move. No Rest

Round Four:

- **Alternate Side Lunges**
- **Dips**
- **Shadow boxing**

Nutrition

Upon Waking:

Have a long glass of warm water with lemon - either fresh lemon or pure lemon dripped in.

12 P.M - Breakfast - Meal One

- 1 x multivitamin
- 2 Whole Eggs Scrambled
- Mixed with Green beans cut up

NUTRITION FACTS

Calories: 409   Fat: 17.6 g   Carbs: 20.6 g   Protein: 16.3 g

4 P.M - Lunch - Meal Two

- 1 Can of Tuna Steak
- Red bell peppers, and low fat Coleslaw

NUTRITION FACTS

Calories: 386   Fat: 17g Carbs: 17g   Protein: 27g

7 P.M - Dinner - Meal Three

- Chicken Breast - With parsley, and bell peppers sliced up
- Peas and Carrots

NUTRITION FACTS

Calories: 318   Fat: 15g   Carbs: 15g   Protein: 24g

The Total Protein intake is 67.3 grams of protein. I would have 1 scoop of protein - 25grams - after your workout making a grand total of 92.3.

Notice how the carbs are minimal - except after your training. You can have carbs then, then stick with veg and fruit.

Tuesday - Cardio

Before Breakfast:

Do 10 minutes of stretches and then go for an early half hour run - outside or use the running machine in a gym.

Be sure to warm down, and remember that you are walking today - do as much as you can.

Nutrition

Upon Waking:

Have a long glass of warm water with lemon - either fresh lemon or pure lemon dripped in.

12 P.M - Breakfast - Meal One

- 1 x multivitamin
- 1 x Whey Protein shake - with peanut butter and a banana
- 1 30gram x Bowl of Granola

NUTRITION FACTS

Calories: 561   Fat: 30.4 g   Carbs: 26.2 g   Protein: 28 g

4 P.M - Lunch - Meal Two

- 1 x Medium sized Tuna Steak
- 1 x Cup Vegetables/salad

NUTRITION FACTS

Calories: 471   Fat: 33.2 g   Carbs: 17 g   Protein: 27 g

7 PM - Dinner - Meal Three

- Tuna Steak
- Rocket and sliced Red Peppers
- Medium Sweet Potato

NUTRITION FACTS

Calories: 456   Fat: 17g Carbs: 29g   Protein: 28g

The Total Protein intake is 83 grams of protein. I would have 1 scoops of protein plus after your workout making a grand total of 108.

Wednesday - Cardio

Cardio

Do this 3 times. Go!

Three circuits: 10 reps per exercise. No rests.

Round One:

- **Burpees**
- **Press-ups**
- **Jumping Jacks**

- **Skipping rope: 3 minutes**

Rest 30 seconds

Three circuits: 20 reps per exercise. No rest

Round Two:

- **Walking Lunges with kettlebell exchange underneath leg**
- **Star jumps**
- **High knees running on the spot**

- **Skipping rope: 5 minutes**

Rest 1 minute

Three circuits: 30 reps per exercise. No rest.

Round Three:

- **Pullups**
- **Box Jumps**
- **Star jumps**

- **Skipping rope: 5 minutes**

Rest 1 minute

Three circuits: 40 reps per move. No Rest

Round Four:

- **Alternate Side Lunges**
- **Dips**
- **Shadow boxing**

Nutrition

Upon Waking:

Have a long glass of warm water with lemon - either fresh lemon or pure lemon dripped in.

12 P.M - Breakfast - Meal One

- 1 x multivitamin
- 2 boiled eggs
- Porridge Oats 30gram serving with 1 tbsp. honey

NUTRITION FACTS

Calories: 409   Fat: 17.6 g   Carbs: 35.6 g   Protein: 20.3 g

4 P.M - Lunch - Meal Two

- Full-Fat Cottage Cheese
- 1 cup Cashews
- 1 Pear
- 1 Banana

NUTRITION FACTS

Calories: 566   Fat: 17 g Carb: 59 g   Protein: 28 g

7 P.M - Dinner - Meal Three

- Pork Chops 5 ounces- with cooked apple - cooked together
- Vegetables 1 cup

NUTRITION FACTS

Calories: 380   Fat: 18.2 g   Carbs: 25 g   Protein: 28 g

The Total Protein intake is 76.3 grams of protein. I would have 1 scoop of protein after your workout making a grand total of 101.3.

Thursday - Cardio

Before Breakfast:

Do 10 minutes of stretches and then go for an early half hour of spinning or a bike ride - outside or use the running machine in a gym.

Or just stick to the pavement and do a 40-minute run. Remember to warm down.

Nutrition

Upon Waking:

Have a long glass of warm water with lemon - either fresh lemon or pure lemon dripped in.

12 P.M - Breakfast - Meal One

- 1 x multivitamin
- 1 x Whey Protein shake - with peanut butter and a banana
- 1 30gram x Bowl of Granola

NUTRITION FACTS

Calories: 561   Fat: 30.4 g   Carbs: 26.2 g   Protein: 28 g

4 P.M Lunch - Meal Two

- 1 x can of Tuna Steak
- Rocket and Beetroot

NUTRITION FACTS

Calories: 471   Fat: 33.2 g   Carbs: 17 g   Protein: 27 g

7 P.M Dinner - Meal Three

- Chicken Breast - With parsley, and bell peppers sliced up
- Steamed Broccoli

NUTRITION FACTS

Calories: 318   Fat: 15g   Carbs: 15g   Protein: 24g

The Total Protein intake is 79 grams of protein. I would have 1 scoops of protein plus after your workout making a grand total of 104.

Friday - Cardio

Cardio

Do this 3 times. Go!

Three circuits: 10 reps per exercise. No rests.

Round One:

- **Burpees**
- **Press-ups**
- **Jumping Jacks**

- **Skipping rope: 5 minutes**

Rest 1 minute

Three circuits: 20 reps per exercise. No rest

Round Two:

- **Walking Lunges with kettlebell exchange underneath leg**
- **Star jumps**
- **High knees running on the spot**

- **Skipping rope: 5 minutes**

Rest 1 minute

Three circuits: 30 reps per exercise. No rest.

Round Three:

- **Pullups**
- **Box Jumps**
- **Star jumps**

- **Skipping rope: 5 minutes**

Rest 1 minute

Three circuits: 40 reps per move. No Rest

Round Four:

- **Alternate Side Lunges**
- **Dips**
- **Shadow boxing**

Nutrition

Upon Waking:

Have a long glass of warm water with lemon - either fresh lemon or pure lemon dripped in.

12 P.M - Breakfast - Meal One

- 1 x multivitamin
- 2 Whole Eggs Scrambled
- Mixed with Green beans cut up

NUTRITION FACTS

Calories: 409   Fat: 17.6 g   Carbs: 20.6 g   Protein: 16.3 g

4 P.M Lunch - Meal Two

- 1 x Medium sized Tuna Steak
- 1 x Cup Vegetables/salad
- 1 Medium sized Baked Potato

NUTRITION FACTS

Calories: 571   Fat: 33.2 g   Carbs: 80 g   Protein: 33 g

7 P.M - Dinner - Meal Three

- Chicken Breast - With parsley, and bell peppers sliced up
- Sprouts - cooked and mashed - add pepper and soft cheese - mash up

NUTRITION FACTS

Calories: 418   Fat: 15g   Carbs: 28g   Protein: 29g

The Total Protein intake is 78.3 grams of protein. I would have 1 scoop of protein - 25grams - after your workout making a grand total of 103.3.

Saturday - Cardio

Before Breakfast

1.5 hours of swimming - or 1 x 50-minute insanity workout.

Remember to warm up before and cool down after.

Nutrition

Upon Waking:

Have a long glass of warm water with lemon - either fresh lemon or pure lemon dripped in.

12 P.M - Breakfast - Meal One

- 1 x multivitamin
- 2 boiled eggs
- Porridge Oats 30gram serving with 1 tbsp. honey

NUTRITION FACTS

Calories: 409   Fat: 17.6 g   Carbs: 35.6 g   Protein: 20.3 g

4 P.M - Lunch - Meal Two

- Full-Fat Cottage Cheese
- 1 cups Cashews
- 1 Apple

NUTRITION FACTS

Calories: 356   Fat: 17 g Carb: 9 g   Protein: 26 g

7 P.M - Dinner - Meal Three

- Pork Chops 5 ounces- with cooked apple - cooked together
- Vegetables 1 cup

NUTRITION FACTS

Calories: 380   Fat: 18.2 g   Carbs: 25 g   Protein: 28 g

The Total Protein intake is 74.3 grams of protein. I would have 1 scoop of protein after your workout making a grand total of 99.3.

Sunday - Rest and Nutrition

We're one week away from the end of our workout! As per usual, relax and enjoy your cheat meal.

Upon Waking:

Have a long glass of warm water with lemon - either fresh lemon or pure lemon dripped in.

Breakfast - Meal One

- 1 x multivitamin
- 3 x scrambled eggs - with spinach
- 1 30gram x Bowl of Granola

NUTRITION FACTS

Calories: 561   Fat: 30.4 g   Carbs: 26.2 g   Protein: 26 g

Lunch - Meal Two

CHEAT MEAL - whatever you fancy!

7 P.M - Dinner - Meal Three

- 1 Cup x Full-Fat Cottage Cheese
- 1 x blob of peanut butter mixed in

NUTRITION FACTS

Calories: 371   Fat: 27 g Carb: 9 g   Protein: 24 g

9. Week 6 Workout

Finally, it's the last week. Let's work hard and make the home stretch count! Quite literally, in this case.

Monday

Warm-up, or meditate, by sitting cross-legged on the floor. Do this after your wake-up water but before breakfast.

Yoga

I have already explained the yoga positions from week 3, so they all apply. For week 6, you're going to try and reach further and hold the positions longer.

Cow and Cat pose – Switch 10 times.
Downward Dog pose – Rise and fall. Repeat 10 times.
Extended Side Angle – Start left leg, then right. Hold for 6 breathers each.

Child's Pose – Hold for 10 breathers.

Rest break of 1 minute

Downward Dog pose – Repeat 10 times

Extended Side Angle – Start left, then right. Hold for 6 breathers each.
Cow and Cat pose – Switch 10 times

Child Pose – Hold for 10 breathers.

Rest for 5 minutes, end session.

Nutrition

Upon Waking:

Have a long glass of warm water with lemon - either fresh lemon or pure lemon dripped in.

12 PM Breakfast – Meal One

- 1 x multivitamin
- An Orange
- Mixed with Green beans cut up

NUTRITION FACTS

Calories: 289   Fat: 4.4 g   Carbs: 34 g   Protein: 5.3 g

4 PM Lunch – Meal Two

- Fruit Salad Cup (Peach, Pear, Apricot, Pineapple, Cherry)
- Frozen Yogurt

NUTRITION FACTS

Calories: 275 Fat: 2.1g Carbs: 49.5g Protein: 21.3g

7 PM Dinner – Meal Three

- Smooth Peanut-Butter Sandwich (2 cups, 2 slices of bread)
- Apple

NUTRITION FACTS

Calories: 442 Fat: 18.3g Carbs: 60.3g Protein: 15.8

Total protein gain is 42.4 g. Again, no protein cups for yoga week.

Tuesday

Meditate cross-legged style for 15 breaths. Do this after the wake-up water but before breakfast.

Yoga

Mountain Pose – 6 breathers, reach higher each time.

Tree Pose – 25 breathers for each leg.
Warrior Pose – 25 breathers for each leg.

Pidgeon Pose – 25 breathers for each leg.

Rest for 1 minute.

Pidgeon Pose – 25 breathers for each leg.

Tree Pose – 25 breathers for each leg.

Mountain Pose – 6 breathers, reach higher each time
Warrior Pose – 25 breathers for each leg.

Rest for 5 minutes, end session.

Nutrition

Upon Waking:

Have a long glass of warm water with lemon - either fresh lemon or pure lemon dripped in.

12 PM Breakfast – Meal One

- 1 x multivitamin
- An Orange
- Mixed with Green beans cut up

NUTRITION FACTS

Calories: 289   Fat: 4.4 g   Carbs: 34 g   Protein: 5.3 g

4 PM Lunch – Meal Two

- Fruit Salad Cup (Peach, Pear, Apricot, Pineapple, Cherry)
- Frozen Yogurt

NUTRITION FACTS

Calories: 275 Fat: 2.1g Carbs: 49.5g Protein: 21.3g

7 PM Dinner – Meal Three

- Smooth Peanut-Butter Sandwich (2 cups, 2 slices of bread)
- Apple

NUTRITION FACTS

Calories: 442 Fat: 18.3g Carbs: 60.3g Protein: 15.8

Total protein gain is 42.4 g.

Wednesday

Meditate cross-legged style for 15 breaths. Do this after wake-up water but before breakfast.

Yoga

Bridge Pose –Hold for 25 breathers.

Cobra Pose – Rise and fall 10 times.

Crow Pose – Hold for 15 breathers.

Seated Twist – 25 breathers for each side.

Rest for 1 minute.

Seated Twist – 25 breathers for each side.

Cobra Pose – Rise and fall 10 times.

Bridge Pose – Hold for 25 breathers.

Crow Pose – Hold for 15 breathers

Nutrition

Upon Waking:

Have a long glass of warm water with lemon - either fresh lemon or pure lemon dripped in.

12 PM Breakfast – Meal One

- 1 x multivitamin
- An Orange
- Porridge Oats 30gram serving with 1 tbsp. honey

NUTRITION FACTS

Calories: 427 Fat: 8.2g   Carbs: 50.2g Protein: 8.9 g

4 P.M - Lunch - Meal Two

- Full-Fat Cottage Cheese
- 1 cups Cashews
- 1 Apple

NUTRITION FACTS

Calories: 356   Fat: 17 g Carb: 9 g   Protein: 26 g

7 PM Dinner – Meal Three

- Canned Tomato Soup
- Full-Fat Cottage Cheese
- Saltine Crackers

NUTRITION FACTS

Calories: 292 Fat: 7.2g Carb: 41g Protein: 18.7g

Total protein gain is 53.6g. Remember not to eat any protein cups this week.

Thursday

Meditate cross-legged style for 15 breaths. Do this after wake-up water but before breakfast.

Yoga

Again, flow and hold the positions for three breaths for each. Once you are done, switch back to the warm-up cross-leg position to rest.

Cow and Cat pose – Switch from Cow to Cat 10 times.
Downward Dog pose – Hold and then switch 10 times
Extended Side Angle – switch legs after 7 breathers
Child's Pose – hold for 10 breaths

Rest break of 1 minute

Downward Dog pose – repeat 10 times

Extended Side Angle – switch legs after 7 breathers
Cow and Cat pose – switch 10 times

Child Pose – hold for 10 breathers.

Rest for 5 minutes, end session.

Nutrition

Upon Waking:

Have a long glass of warm water with lemon - either fresh lemon or pure lemon dripped in.

12 PM Breakfast – Meal One

- 1 x multivitamin
- An Orange
- Mixed with Green beans cut up

NUTRITION FACTS

Calories: 289   Fat: 4.4 g   Carbs: 34 g   Protein: 5.3 g

4 PM Lunch – Meal Two

- Fruit Salad Cup (Peach, Pear, Apricot, Pineapple, Cherry)
- Frozen Yogurt

NUTRITION FACTS

Calories: 275 Fat: 2.1g Carbs: 49.5g Protein: 21.3g

7 PM Dinner – Meal Three

- Smooth Peanut-Butter Sandwich (2 cups, 2 slices of bread)
- Apple

NUTRITION FACTS

Calories: 442 Fat: 18.3g Carbs: 60.3g Protein: 15.8

Total protein gain is 42.4g.

Friday

Meditate cross-legged style for 15 breaths. Do this after wake-up water but before breakfast.

Seated Twist – 25 breathers for each side.
Pidgeon Pose – 25 breathers per leg.
Downward Dog – repeat 10 times.
Child Pose – hold for 10 breathers.

Rest for 1 minute.

Pidgeon Pose – 25 breathers per leg.
Downward Dog – repeat 10 times.
Seated Twist – 25 breathers for each side.

Child Pose – hold for 10 breathers.

Rest for 5 minutes. End session.

Nutrition

Upon Waking:

Have a long glass of warm water with lemon - either fresh lemon or pure lemon dripped in.

12 PM Breakfast – Meal One

- 1 x multivitamin
- An Orange
- Porridge Oats 30gram serving with 1 tbsp. honey

NUTRITION FACTS

Calories: 427 Fat: 8.2 g   Carbs: 50.2g Protein: 8.9 g

4 PM Lunch – Meal Two

- Full-Fat Cottage Cheese
- 1 cups Cashews
- 1 Apple

NUTRITION FACTS

Calories: 356   Fat: 17 g Carb: 9 g   Protein: 26 g

7 PM Dinner – Meal Three

- Smooth Peanut-Butter Sandwich (2 cups, 2 slices of bread)
- Apple

NUTRITION FACTS

Calories: 442 Fat: 18.3g Carbs: 60.3g Protein: 15.8

Total protein gain is 50.7g

Saturday

Tree Pose – 15 breathers for each leg.

Extended Side Angle – switch legs between 3 breathers
Mountain Pose – 3 breathers, reach higher each time

Warrior Pose – 15 breathers for each leg.

Rest for 1 minute.

Mountain Pose – 3 breathers, reach higher each time.
Warrior Pose – 15 breathers for each leg.

Extended Side Angle – switch legs between 3 breathers.

Tree Pose – 15 breathers for each leg

Rest for 5 minutes. End session.

Nutrition

Upon Waking:

Have a long glass of warm water with lemon - either fresh lemon or pure lemon dripped in.

12 P.M - Breakfast - Meal One

- 1 x multivitamin
- An Orange
- Porridge Oats 30gram serving with 1 tbsp. honey

NUTRITION FACTS

Calories: 427 Fat: 8.2g   Carbs: 50.2g Protein: 8.9 g

4 P.M - Lunch - Meal Two

- Full-Fat Cottage Cheese
- 1 cups Cashews
- 1 Apple

NUTRITION FACTS

Calories: 356   Fat: 17 g Carb: 9 g   Protein: 26 g

7 P.M Dinner

- Canned Tomato Soup
- Full-Fat Cottage Cheese
- Saltine Crackers

NUTRITION FACTS

Calories: 292 Fat: 7.2g Carb: 41g Protein: 18.7g

Total protein gain is 53.6g

Sunday - Rest and Nutrition

You did it! You finished all 6 weeks of your Intermittent Fasting diet workout!

By now your body should be strong as an ox, pumped as a dog, and limber as a snake. From here your workout routine should be smooth sailing, whether you want to keep pushing yourself or not. As a reward for your diligence and persistence, you'll get THREE cheat meals this time!

Upon Waking:

Have a long glass of warm water with lemon - either fresh lemon or pure lemon dripped in.

Breakfast - Meal One

CHEAT MEAL – whatever you fancy!

Lunch - Meal Two

CHEAT MEAL - whatever you fancy!

Dinner - Meal

CHEAT MEAL - whatever you fancy!

Conclusion: Final Notes, Cheats and the Number 1 thing to do!

CONGRATULATIONS!

Thank for you purchasing this Book, and congratulations on finishing all 6 weeks!

I hope this book is helping you reach your best. If you deviated or missed the odd day, don't worry, in the scheme of things you have taken steps to improve yourself. In fact in the first few weeks I expect you to take the odd day off. It's tough and is designed that way, especially the last 3 weeks. The important thing is not to overdo it. Learn about your body. Learn when to ease off for a day or two. Also learn when to push. Now we recover and rest and go again with a renewed determination to do better than before.

Fitness isn't about one workout or one meal. It's about you committing to the long term to improve yourself. That's all, and by saying I'm going to do this, you have made the first step.

Strive to improve your form for your weights workouts, feel the muscles contract, feel the burn. Use light weights to begin with and feel the right muscles working. This is a huge element and many people use too big a weight and end up training the wrong muscles. Make sure you complete your cardio - this is the real fat burner.

I keep checking my pedometer on my phone to see how many steps I've taken I always strive for more than 6000 every day. So that's around 1 hour of walking. I always park further away than I need to, and I try to walk every morning. This adds to your cardio goals - so go for it - every little extra counts.

Try to keep to your nutrition. Don't trick yourself after a workout into thinking 'I've earnt that chocolate bar or pizza'. You can have those on your cheat days.

In terms of your Intermittent Fasting, I've put 4pm for your lunch, is this possible for you? If not move it to 5pm or

6:30pm. Make my plan work for you. You are in control and this is a guide that you should use to your advantage. You may need to adjust your nutrition adding more protein, adding more carbs before training. You need to get to know how your body responds. If you feel hungry or lethargic increase your healthy food intake a little. You may feel like you're not leaning up, in which case have smaller meals. Reduce your calories.

Keep using the 16 8 Intermittent Fasting routine if you can. Let it last for a month and see how you feel. It won't work wonders in days, it'll take time. And remember it only works when you completely fast for 16 hours - no food at all. Drink plenty of water.

There'll be hard times when you're tired or just want to chill, it's up to you to know when to push on and do that workout or just take a break. Even a 30 minute walk in the evening is better than nothing.

As I said in terms of training you may struggle at first. I would reduce sets - not workouts. Keep to the schedule, keep working the muscles regularly and you will get results.

Number 1 thing to do:

Take a picture before any training, this is what you want to improve. Then take a picture every 2 weeks to see how you're progressing.

This is fun, it's taking up a portion of your life for the good, so it should never feel like a chore!

There are a number of cheats I use to maximize muscles gain in terms of supplements.

- A weights Post workout shake is a given - 25grams of Whey Isolate is minimum which will help you recover.
- A scoop of BCAA's in 500ml of water pre-workout and something to sip. Again have this post workout. This is

great for recovery and getting you back to feeling normal.

Remember fitness and staying fit is about getting to know your body and only you can become the ultimate expert on that front!

Finally, I have included a number of other book's I've written that you may find useful on fitness and also a number of great diet books and other fitness books that are a great read. And be sure to review this book and the others listed here on Amazon.com!

So there we have it - you will be on your way to getting that amazing body - have a go, enjoy the workouts and be the change! Good luck!

These Books Could Also Assist you with your Fitness Goals:

<u>Vegetarian Bodybuilding Nutrition: How To Crack The Muscle Building Success Code With Vegetarian Bodybuilding Nutrition</u>

<u>How To Build Massive Shoulders</u>: 6 Week Workout for Massive Shoulders

Made in the USA
Middletown, DE
18 October 2023

41040963R00066